CAITLIN CLARK MEMOIR

How She Became Every Defender's Worst Fear

JANET D. ROSS

Caitlin Clark Memoir © 2025 by JANET D. ROSS

ALL RIGHTS RESERVED

No part of this book may be reproduced, distributed, or transmitted in any form or by any means without the prior written permission of the publisher, except in the case of brief quotations embodied in critical reviews and certain other noncommercial uses permitted by copyright law.

DISCLAIMER

This book is an unauthorized biography of Caitlin Clark. The information contained within is based on publicly available sources, interviews, and the author's personal perspective as a fan of Caitlin Clark's career. The book is not officially endorsed or approved by Caitlin Clark, her family, or any associated parties. All views, opinions, and interpretations are solely those of the author and do not reflect the opinions of Caitlin Clark herself. The purpose of this biography is to celebrate Caitlin Clark's impact on basketball and the legacy she is building, rather than to claim exclusive or personal insight into her private life.

Contents

INTRODUCTION 1

FAQs 5
    Quick Answers About Caitlin Clark's Life & Career 5

List of Awards & Records 9
    The Accolades That Cemented Her Legacy 9

CHAPTER 1 13
    Early Life 13

CHAPTER 2 17
    High School Dominance to College Stardom 17

CHAPTER 3 21
    Breaking Records & Shaping Women's Basketball 21

CHAPTER 4 25
    The People Behind the Superstar 25

CHAPTER 5 29
    The Adversities That Fueled Her Fire 29

CHAPTER 6 34

Net Worth & Endorsements – The Business of Being Caitlin Clark 34

CHAPTER 7 40

How She Changed the Game Forever 40

Author's Perspective 46

Why Caitlin Clark's Story Matters 46

This page intentionally left blank

JANET D. ROSS
Caitlin Clark Memoir

INTRODUCTION

Who is Caitlin Clark to you? A once-in-a-generation talent? A fearless competitor who has changed the game? A nightmare for defenders who dares them to stop her, only to leave them hopeless? Or maybe she's just another basketball player, someone you've only heard about but never truly followed.

For me, Caitlin Clark is much more than that. She's a force, a symbol of what is possible when talent meets relentless hard work. From the first time I saw her play, I knew she was different. There was something about the way she carried herself on the court—the confidence, the fire, the way she shot the ball as if she was born to do it. It wasn't just skill. It was something deeper. A hunger. A purpose.

This is an unauthorized biography. Caitlin Clark didn't sit down with me to tell her story. She didn't approve this book, nor did she ask for it to be written. But I wrote it anyway because I couldn't help myself. Some stories demand to be told, and hers is one of them.

Growing up, I had a dream—a big, impossible dream—to be like her. Maybe you had a dream like that, too. To play at the highest level, to be the best, to stand out in a way that made the world take notice. For me, basketball was everything. I lived for the sound of sneakers squeaking on the hardwood, for the thrill of a perfect shot swishing through the net. I spent hours on the court, imagining myself making game-winning shots, just like the ones Caitlin Clark has hit over and over again.

But dreams and reality don't always align. Some of us get there, and some of us don't. I never became the player I once believed I could be, but Caitlin did. She didn't just make it—she dominated. And in doing so, she became the kind of player people talk about for years, the kind that changes the way the game is played.

Caitlin Clark is a name that now echoes through gyms, sports networks, and locker rooms across the country. She has become the face of women's college basketball, a sharpshooter with ice in her veins and a confidence that never wavers. She doesn't just score; she shatters records. She doesn't just play; she takes over. When she steps onto the court, people expect something extraordinary to happen, and most of the time, it does.

But beyond the stats, beyond the deep three-pointers and the flashy passes, there's a story—a story of a girl who fell in love with basketball and refused to settle for anything less than greatness. That's what this book is about.

Some people might say she's cocky, too confident, too bold for her own good. But isn't that what makes a legend? The best players, the ones who leave their mark, don't apologize for being great. They don't shrink themselves to make others comfortable. Caitlin Clark has never played small. She has never been afraid to take the big shot, to call for the ball, to be the one who decides the game.

This book isn't just about her success—it's about the journey. The work, the failures, the pressure, the moments of doubt. It's about the way she kept going, even when the world doubted her. Because if there's one thing you should know about Caitlin Clark, it's that she doesn't back down.

There was a time when women's basketball didn't get the attention it deserved. Players like Caitlin Clark have changed that. She has brought a new level of excitement to the game, forcing people to pay attention. She fills arenas. She breaks records. She proves, night after night, that women's basketball is just as thrilling, just as intense, just as worthy of the spotlight as any other sport.

Maybe you're reading this book because you're already a fan, someone who has followed her journey from the beginning. Or maybe you're here out of curiosity, wondering what all the hype is about. Either way, by the time you reach the last page, you'll understand why Caitlin Clark isn't just another basketball player.

She is the kind of athlete who only comes around once in a lifetime. The kind that makes you believe in the impossible. The kind that makes you wish, even just for a moment, that you could step into her shoes and feel what it's like to be that fearless, that unstoppable, that great.

This is her story.

FAQS

Quick Answers About Caitlin Clark's Life & Career

Caitlin Clark is one of the most talked-about basketball players of her generation. Her talent, confidence, and ability to take over a game have made her a fan favorite, but they've also sparked a lot of curiosity. Fans, analysts, and even casual sports watchers have plenty of questions about her life, career, and future. Here are some of the most frequently asked questions—and their answers.

1. Where was Caitlin Clark born?
Caitlin Clark was born in Des Moines, Iowa, on January 22, 2002. She grew up in West Des Moines, where she developed her love for basketball.

2. What high school did Caitlin Clark attend?
She attended Dowling Catholic High School in West Des Moines, Iowa, where she became a basketball sensation and one of the top recruits in the country.

3. Why did Caitlin Clark choose to play for Iowa instead of other top programs?
Despite receiving offers from powerhouse schools like Notre Dame, Texas, and Oregon, Clark chose Iowa because of its strong women's basketball program, the opportunity to play close to home, and the chance to be a key player from the start.

4. What position does Caitlin Clark play?
She primarily plays as a point guard but is known for her

versatility, ability to score at all three levels, and elite playmaking skills.

5. What is Caitlin Clark's playing style?
She is known for her deep three-point shooting, court vision, and aggressive scoring mentality. Many compare her style to NBA players like Stephen Curry because of her long-range shots and quick decision-making.

6. Has Caitlin Clark ever played for Team USA?
Yes, she has represented the United States in international competitions. She played for Team USA in the FIBA U19 Women's World Cup, where she helped the team win gold.

7. What records has Caitlin Clark broken in college?
She has set numerous records, including becoming the fastest player in NCAA women's basketball history to reach 2,000 career points. She has also led the nation in scoring and assists multiple times.

8. What are Caitlin Clark's career-high stats in a single game?
One of her most impressive performances came when she scored over 40 points in a game while also dishing out double-digit assists. Her ability to dominate both as a scorer and playmaker makes her one of the most complete players in the game.

9. How does Caitlin Clark handle pressure on the court?
Clark thrives under pressure. She embraces big moments, often calling for the ball in clutch situations. Her confidence and ability to perform in high-stakes games have made her a leader for Iowa.

10. Who are Caitlin Clark's biggest rivals?
While she respects all competitors, some of her most talked-about matchups have been against other top-tier players like

Paige Bueckers from UConn and Aliyah Boston, formerly of South Carolina.

11. Has Caitlin Clark faced criticism in her career?
Yes. Some critics claim she is too emotional or too bold in her approach to the game. However, many fans and analysts admire her fiery competitiveness and believe it's part of what makes her great.

12. What does Caitlin Clark's training routine look like?
Clark is known for her intense work ethic. She spends hours in the gym perfecting her shooting, conditioning, and playmaking. She also focuses on strength training to improve her endurance and ability to handle physical play.

13. What is Caitlin Clark's impact on women's basketball?
She has drawn national attention to the sport, increasing viewership and proving that women's college basketball can be just as exciting as men's. Her presence alone has helped fill arenas and create new fans of the game.

14. Is Caitlin Clark planning to enter the WNBA?
While she is expected to enter the WNBA draft, the exact timing depends on her personal and career goals. Many believe she will be a high draft pick and a future WNBA star.

15. Does Caitlin Clark have endorsement deals?
Yes. With the rise of NIL (Name, Image, and Likeness) deals, Clark has signed endorsement contracts with major brands, further proving her influence in the sport.

16. What is Caitlin Clark's net worth?
While the exact figure is unclear, Clark has earned a significant amount through NIL deals, sponsorships, and her basketball career. Her value is expected to rise even more if she joins the WNBA.

17. Does Caitlin Clark have social media?
Yes. She is active on platforms like Instagram and Twitter, where she shares moments from her career, endorsements, and personal life updates.

18. What does Caitlin Clark do outside of basketball?
When she's not playing, she enjoys spending time with family and friends, and she often engages in community outreach programs. She has also shown support for growing women's sports beyond basketball.

19. What are Caitlin Clark's future goals?
While she has not publicly outlined every goal, it is clear that she aims to continue making an impact in basketball—whether at the college, professional, or international level.

20. What makes Caitlin Clark different from other players?
Her combination of confidence, deep shooting range, playmaking ability, and leadership sets her apart. She is not just a scorer—she is a game-changer who makes those around her better.

LIST OF AWARDS & RECORDS

The Accolades That Cemented Her Legacy

Caitlin Clark's basketball journey has been nothing short of historic. From her high school days to her dominance at the college level, she has set records, won prestigious awards, and redefined what it means to be an elite player. Every step of the way, she has left her mark, breaking barriers and proving that she belongs among the greatest to ever play the game.

Her trophy cabinet is already overflowing, and she's not even done yet. Whether it's individual accolades, team achievements, or jaw-dropping statistics, Caitlin Clark has built a legacy that will be talked about for generations. Here's a look at some of her most significant awards and records.

High School Honors

Before she even stepped onto the college court, Caitlin Clark was already a national star. Her performances at Dowling Catholic High School made her one of the most highly recruited players in the country.

- **McDonald's All-American (2020)** – Recognized as one of the top high school players in the nation.
- **Gatorade Iowa Girls Basketball Player of the Year (2020)** – Given to the best high school basketball player in the state.
- **Nike Hoop Summit Selection (2020)** – A prestigious invitation for elite high school players.

- **No. 4 Ranked Player in the 2020 Recruiting Class** – According to ESPN, making her one of the most sought-after recruits in the country.

College Achievements & Awards

Once she arrived at the University of Iowa, Clark wasted no time proving she was a generational talent. From her freshman year onward, she dominated the college basketball scene, collecting awards and breaking records along the way.

- **NCAA Women's Scoring Leader (Multiple Seasons)** – Led the entire nation in points per game.
- **Big Ten Player of the Year (Multiple Times)** – The best player in one of the most competitive conferences in women's college basketball.
- **AP National Player of the Year (2023, 2024)** – Recognized as the best player in the country.
- **John R. Wooden Award (2023, 2024)** – Given to the most outstanding college basketball player in the country.
- **Naismith College Player of the Year (2023, 2024)** – One of the most prestigious individual awards in college basketball.
- **Nancy Lieberman Award (2022, 2023, 2024)** – Recognizing the best point guard in women's college basketball.
- **First-Team All-American (Multiple Times)** – Selected as one of the best five players in the nation.
- **Big Ten Freshman of the Year (2021)** – A standout first season that made her one of the most exciting young players in the country.
- **NCAA Tournament Record – Most Points in a Single Game** – Showcasing her ability to take over on the biggest stage.
- **First Player in NCAA History (Men's or Women's) with 900+ Points and 300+ Assists in a Season** – A remarkable stat that highlights her all-around dominance.

- **Fastest Player to Reach 2,000 Career Points in NCAA Women's Basketball** – Proving her scoring ability is at a historic level.

Records That Redefined Women's College Basketball

Caitlin Clark hasn't just won awards—she's rewritten the record books. Her ability to score, pass, and lead has placed her among the all-time greats. Here are some of the jaw-dropping records she has set:

- **All-Time Leading Scorer in Iowa Women's Basketball History** – Cementing her place as a Hawkeye legend.
- **Most Three-Pointers in a Single NCAA Season** – Her deep shooting ability is unlike anything the game has seen before.
- **Most 40-Point Games in NCAA Women's Basketball History** – Consistently dominating in high-pressure matchups.
- **Only Player in NCAA History with Back-to-Back Triple-Doubles in the NCAA Tournament** – Showing her ability to impact the game in every way.
- **First Division I Women's Player to Record 3,000+ Points, 900+ Assists, and 800+ Rebounds in a Career** – A true testament to her versatility.
- **Most Points Scored in a Single Women's NCAA Tournament** – Delivering when it matters most.

Impact on the Game & Cultural Influence

Beyond the numbers and awards, Caitlin Clark's influence goes far beyond the basketball court. She has drawn national attention to women's basketball, filled arenas, and helped change the perception of the sport.

- **Set a New Women's College Basketball Viewership Record** – Her games have broken TV ratings records, proving that women's basketball is thriving.
- **Helped Iowa Set Multiple Attendance Records** – Fans pack the stands just to watch her play.
- **One of the Highest NIL Valuations in College Sports** – Her marketability and star power have made her one of the biggest names in college athletics.

With everything she has already accomplished, one question remains—what's next for Caitlin Clark? Will she continue breaking records at the college level, or will she take her talents to the WNBA and make an impact at the professional level? Wherever she goes, one thing is certain—she will continue to inspire and amaze.

Caitlin Clark has already built a legacy that will stand the test of time. The records may one day be broken, and new stars will emerge, but her impact on the game is permanent. She has changed the way people see women's basketball, and for that, she will always be remembered.

CHAPTER 1

EARLY LIFE

Caitlin Clark's journey to basketball stardom began long before she donned a college jersey or shattered records on the national stage. Her early life in West Des Moines, Iowa, was steeped in a rich tapestry of family support, diverse interests, and formative experiences that shaped her into the formidable athlete she is today.

Born on January 22, 2002, in Des Moines, Iowa, Caitlin is the second of three children to Brent and Anne Nizzi-Clark. Her father, Brent, was a dual-sport athlete at Simpson College, excelling in both basketball and baseball. Reflecting on his daughter's passion, Brent once remarked, "I see a lot of myself at times in Caitlin in terms of her passion for the game." Anne, Caitlin's mother, comes from a lineage deeply rooted in sports; her father, Bob Nizzi, served as a football coach and school administrator at Dowling Catholic High School in West Des Moines. This familial connection to athletics created an environment where sports were not just activities but integral to daily life.

Growing up alongside her older brother, Blake, and younger brother, Colin, Caitlin was immersed in a world of constant competition and camaraderie. Blake, who later played football at Iowa State University, recalled their childhood games: "We were always involved in sports... when you're just around something that much, it's what you do, too." These backyard battles were more than just play; they were the crucible in which Caitlin's competitive spirit was forged. Colin recounted a particularly intense moment: "There was a loose ball, and she ended up shoving me... into the wall. Split my head open. Got four staples." Such incidents, while painful, underscored the fierce determination that would become Caitlin's hallmark.

The Clark household was a hub of athletic activity, with evenings often spent attending local games or watching sports together. This constant exposure nurtured Caitlin's love for various sports. She dabbled in softball, volleyball, soccer, tennis, and golf, showcasing a versatile athleticism. However, basketball emerged as her true passion. At the tender age of five, Caitlin began playing basketball, often competing in boys' recreational leagues due to limited opportunities for young girls. Her father, Brent, coached her during these early years, instilling fundamental skills and a deep understanding of the game. He emphasized the importance of passion, noting, "All in all, that's really what drives her and makes her the player that she is."

A defining moment in Caitlin's early basketball journey occurred during a boys' league game in Waukee when she was just five years old. Facing a particularly aggressive opponent, young Caitlin found herself overwhelmed and in tears. Her father, serving as her coach, took her aside to console her. After regaining her composure, Caitlin re-entered the game with renewed determination. Instead of shying away, she confronted the bully head-on, delivering a decisive block that sent him out of bounds. Her grandfather, Bob Nizzi, who witnessed the event, recalled, "She went right to this guy and put on the best downfield block that I have ever seen... She's a five-year-old little girl. And that is when her grandmother and I looked at each other and said, 'She's going to be really something.'" This incident not only showcased her resilience but also hinted at the tenacity that would define her future career.

Beyond the family dynamics, Caitlin's involvement in the community played a pivotal role in her development. In sixth grade, she joined the All Iowa Attack, an Amateur Athletic Union (AAU) basketball program based in Ames, Iowa. Competing against older players, Caitlin honed her skills and developed a competitive edge. The program's rigorous training and exposure to high-level competition prepared her for the challenges ahead. Her time with All Iowa Attack also fostered lasting friendships and a sense of community, reinforcing the values of teamwork and perseverance.

While basketball was a central focus, Caitlin's parents ensured she led a balanced life. They encouraged her to explore various interests and maintained a supportive yet grounded environment. This approach prevented burnout and allowed Caitlin to cultivate a genuine love for the game. Reflecting on her upbringing, Caitlin has expressed gratitude for her family's unwavering support and the freedom to pursue her passions without undue pressure.

Caitlin's early experiences were not limited to the basketball court. She was an active participant in her community, attending local events and engaging in various extracurricular activities. These experiences broadened her horizons and instilled a sense of responsibility and connection to her roots. Traveling for AAU tournaments and family vacations exposed her to diverse cultures and environments, fostering adaptability and a broader worldview.

Emotionally, Caitlin's formative years were marked by a journey of self-discovery. The challenges she faced, both on and off the court, taught her resilience and the importance of mental fortitude. Her family's emphasis on moral and ethical values instilled a strong sense of right and wrong, guiding her actions and decisions. This foundation has been evident in her sportsmanship and leadership qualities, earning her respect both as a player and an individual.

The environment in which Caitlin was raised also played a significant role in shaping her character. West Des Moines, with its close-knit community and rich sporting culture, provided ample opportunities for growth and development. Access to parks, recreational facilities, and a supportive community nurtured her athletic pursuits and personal growth. The values of hard work, humility, and community engagement prevalent in her surroundings became integral to her identity.

CHAPTER 2

HIGH SCHOOL DOMINANCE TO COLLEGE STARDOM

Caitlin Clark's basketball journey is a testament to relentless dedication, exceptional talent, and an unyielding competitive spirit. From her early days at Dowling Catholic High School to her record-breaking tenure at the University of Iowa, Clark has consistently demonstrated her prowess on the court, earning her a place among the elite in women's basketball.

At Dowling Catholic High School in West Des Moines, Iowa, Clark's impact was immediate and profound. As a freshman, she averaged 15.3 points, 4.7 assists, and 2.3 steals per game, showcasing her versatility and court awareness. Her performance earned her Class 5A All-State third-team honors from the Iowa Newspaper Association and an All-Iowa honorable mention from The Des Moines Register. Reflecting on her early days, Clark once said, "I always wanted to be the best, no matter the stage or the competition."

Clark's sophomore year saw a significant leap in her performance. She averaged 27.1 points, 6.5 rebounds, 4 assists, and 2.3 steals per game, ranking second in the state for scoring. Her remarkable play led Dowling to a 20–4 record and a spot in the Class 5A state quarterfinals. For her efforts, she was named to the first-team Class 5A All-State by the Iowa Print Sports Writers Association (IPSWA) and honored as the Central Iowa Metro League Player of the Year by The Des Moines Register.

One of the most memorable moments of Clark's high school career occurred during her junior year. On February 4, 2019, she delivered a historic performance by scoring 60 points in a 90–78 victory over Mason City High School. This feat marked the second-highest single-game point total in Iowa's five-on-five girls' basketball history and set a state record with 13 three-pointers made in a single game. Reflecting on that game, Clark mentioned, "I was just in the zone; every shot felt right." Her junior year statistics were equally impressive, leading the state with an average of 32.6 points, along with 6.8 rebounds, 3.6 assists, and 2.3 steals per game. These achievements earned her the Iowa Gatorade Player of the Year award and a repeat selection to the IPSWA Class 5A All-State first team.

In her senior year, Clark continued to dominate, averaging 33.4 points, 8 rebounds, 4 assists, and 2.7 steals per game, once again leading the state in scoring. Under her leadership, Dowling achieved a 19–4 record and advanced to the Class 5A regional final. By the end of her high school career, Clark had amassed 2,547 points, placing her fourth on Iowa's all-time five-on-five scoring list. Her outstanding performance garnered her several accolades, including a second Iowa Gatorade Player of the Year award, the Des Moines Register All-Iowa Athlete of the Year, and the prestigious Iowa Miss Basketball title. She was also selected for the McDonald's All-American Game and the Jordan Brand Classic, though both events were canceled due to the COVID-19 pandemic.

Transitioning to college, Clark committed to the University of Iowa, drawn by the team's fast-paced offense and the opportunity to make an immediate impact. Her freshman season in 2020–2021 was nothing short of spectacular. Clark led the nation in scoring with an average of 26.6 points per game and was second in assists, averaging 7.1 per game. Her dynamic play earned her the Big Ten Freshman of the Year award and a unanimous selection to the All-Big Ten first team. Reflecting on her transition to college basketball, Clark stated, "The speed and physicality were a step up, but I embraced the challenge."

Clark's sophomore season saw her elevate her game even further. She averaged 27 points, 8 assists, and 7 rebounds per game, leading Iowa to a Big Ten Tournament championship and a deep run in the NCAA Tournament. Her exceptional performance earned her the prestigious Naismith College Player of the Year award, recognizing her as the nation's top player. "Winning the Naismith was a dream come true, but it also motivated me to keep improving," Clark remarked.

In her junior year, Clark continued to break records and set new standards. She became the fastest player in NCAA Division I history, male or female, to reach 2,000 career points. Her averages of 28.4 points, 8.2 assists, and 7.1 rebounds per game not only led her team but also placed her among the top performers nationally. Clark's ability to consistently deliver triple-doubles and her knack for clutch performances solidified her reputation as a generational talent.

Off the court, Clark's influence grew as she became a prominent figure in collegiate athletics. She actively engaged in community service, participated in youth basketball clinics, and used her platform to advocate for women's sports. Her leadership extended beyond the basketball court, inspiring young athletes to pursue their dreams with determination and resilience.

As Clark's college career progressed, she continued to amass accolades and break records. She led the Iowa Hawkeyes to multiple NCAA Tournament appearances, including a historic run to the Final Four in her senior year. Her performance in the tournament was nothing short of extraordinary, recording multiple 40-point games and showcasing her ability to perform under pressure. Reflecting on the journey, Clark said, "Every game, every practice, was a step toward our goal. The support of my teammates and coaches made it all possible."

By the end of her collegiate career, Clark had etched her name into the annals of basketball history. She became the all-time leading scorer in NCAA Division I history, surpassing both men's and women's records with a total of 3,951 points. Her jersey, number 22, was retired by the University of Iowa, a testament to her monumental impact on the program. "Having my jersey

CHAPTER 3

BREAKING RECORDS & SHAPING WOMEN'S BASKETBALL

Caitlin Clark has become a transformative figure in women's basketball, leaving an indelible mark through her record-breaking performances and significant contributions to the sport. Her journey from a promising high school athlete to a professional star in the WNBA has been marked by numerous achievements and accolades, reflecting her dedication and impact on the game.

In her sophomore year at the University of Iowa, Clark led the nation with an average of 27.0 points and 8.0 assists per game. She also topped the charts in total assists (257), total points (863), free throws made (200), triple-doubles (5), and 30-point games (11). This remarkable feat made her the only Division I women's basketball player to lead the country in both assists and points per game in a single season.

Clark's exceptional performance did not go unnoticed. She was honored with several prestigious awards, including the AP Player of the Year, the Honda Sports Award, the John R. Wooden Award, Naismith College Player of the Year, USBWA National Player of the Year, and the Wade Trophy. These accolades recognized her as the nation's top player and highlighted her significant contributions to her team's success.

Transitioning to the professional arena, Clark was selected as the first overall pick by the Indiana Fever in the 2024 WNBA Draft. Her rookie season was nothing short of spectacular. She earned the WNBA Rookie of the Year award and was named to the All-WNBA First Team. Clark also led the league in assists, securing the WNBA Peak Performer Award.

Beyond her on-court achievements, Clark's influence has extended to increasing the visibility and popularity of women's basketball. Her dynamic playing style and charismatic presence have attracted a broader audience, leading to higher viewership and attendance for the games she participates in. This phenomenon, often referred to as the "Caitlin Clark effect," has played a pivotal role in elevating the profile of women's sports.

Clark's impact is further underscored by her recognition as the AP Female Athlete of the Year and TIME Athlete of the Year in 2024. These honors reflect not only her athletic excellence but also her role in shaping the cultural landscape of sports. In an interview, Clark expressed her feelings about the attention, stating, "I feel like the most controversial person," highlighting the intense media focus and discussions surrounding her career.

Her influence has also been acknowledged by peers across different sports. NFL star Joe Burrow praised Clark's skills and expressed admiration for her performances, indicating the widespread respect she commands in the athletic community.

Clark's contributions extend beyond her personal achievements. She has been a vocal advocate for recognizing the contributions of Black players in the league, emphasizing the importance of appreciating and investing in the players who have been instrumental in building the league's foundation. Clark stated, "A lot of those players in the league that have been really good have been Black players. This league has kind of been built on them."

In summary, Caitlin Clark's career is a testament to her exceptional talent, dedication, and the profound impact she has had on women's basketball. Her achievements have not only redefined records but have also played a crucial role in elevating the sport's status in society and culture. As she continues her journey, Clark remains a pivotal figure, inspiring future generations and contributing to the growth and recognition of women's sports.

CHAPTER 4

THE PEOPLE BEHIND THE SUPERSTAR

Caitlin Clark's meteoric rise in the world of basketball is not solely attributed to her exceptional talent and dedication; it is deeply rooted in the unwavering support and influence of her family, close relationships, and personal interests. Beyond the basketball court, Clark's personal life is a testament to the strong bonds and values that have shaped her into the remarkable individual she is today.

Born on January 22, 2002, in Des Moines, Iowa, Caitlin is the second of three children to Brent and Anne Nizzi-Clark. Her father, Brent, is a sales executive at Concentric International and was a dual-sport athlete at Simpson College, excelling in both basketball and baseball. Reflecting on her father's influence, Caitlin has often mentioned, "My dad always pushed me to be the best version of myself, both on and off the court." Her mother, Anne, of Italian descent, is a former marketing executive and the daughter of Bob Nizzi, a revered football coach at Dowling Catholic High School. This rich athletic lineage provided Caitlin with a nurturing environment where sports and discipline were integral to daily life.

Growing up in West Des Moines, Caitlin shared her home with two brothers: an older brother, Blake, and a younger brother, Colin. Blake played college football for Iowa State, while Colin pursued his own athletic interests. The sibling dynamic was both competitive and supportive. Caitlin recalls, "Playing with my brothers toughened me up. They never took it easy on me, and that made me the competitor I am today."

Family gatherings often revolved around sports, fostering a sense of camaraderie and healthy competition.

The Nizzi family, on her mother's side, has deep roots in the Dowling Catholic community. Her grandfather, Bob Nizzi, served as a football coach and athletic director at Dowling Catholic High School. Caitlin's aunt, Kathy, and uncle, Tom, also attended Dowling, with Tom playing basketball alongside sportswriter Pat Harty. Harty reminisces, "The Nizzi family was well-known within the Dowling community long before Caitlin Clark burst on the scene." This legacy instilled in Caitlin a profound sense of pride and responsibility toward her community.

Despite her burgeoning fame, Caitlin has always prioritized her personal relationships. In April 2023, she began dating Connor McCaffery, a fellow University of Iowa athlete who played both basketball and baseball. Their shared experiences as student-athletes created a strong bond. Connor, the son of Iowa men's basketball head coach Fran McCaffery, has been a steadfast supporter of Caitlin's career. On their one-year anniversary in April 2024, Connor shared a heartfelt message on social media, referring to Caitlin as his "queen" and expressing pride in her accomplishments. Their relationship exemplifies mutual respect and understanding, with Caitlin noting, "Having someone who understands the demands of being a student-athlete has been invaluable."

Beyond her basketball career, Caitlin has a diverse range of interests. An avid golfer since childhood, she often turns to the sport as a form of relaxation and mental rejuvenation. In November 2024, she participated in a pro-am tournament at the Pelican Golf Club in Florida, competing alongside top golfers like Nelly Korda and Annika Sörenstam. Reflecting on the experience, Caitlin said, "Golf offers a different kind of challenge. It's a mental game, and it helps me unwind." Her boyfriend, Connor, played a pivotal role in refining her golf skills, helping her discover that her right eye is dominant—a revelation that improved her game.

Caitlin's interests also extend to the culinary arts. She finds solace in baking, with a particular fondness for crafting brownies. This hobby serves as a therapeutic escape from the rigors of her athletic schedule. She shares, "Baking is my way to relax. There's something comforting about creating something sweet from scratch." This passion for baking not only provides personal joy but also allows her to share delightful moments with family and friends.

Faith plays a central role in Caitlin's life. Raised in the Catholic Church, she is a parishioner at St. Francis of Assisi Catholic Church in Des Moines. Her time at Dowling Catholic High School reinforced her spiritual foundation. Caitlin attributes the school's "special culture" to its emphasis on prayer and the ability to "live our faith every day." This spiritual grounding has been a source of strength and guidance throughout her career.

Despite her soaring career, Caitlin remains deeply connected to her roots. She has been a lifelong fan of the Chicago Cubs and has had the honor of throwing out the first pitch for both the major league team and its Triple-A affiliate, the Iowa Cubs. Additionally, she supports the Kansas City Chiefs and made history by appearing on the ManningCast for a Monday Night Football game featuring the Chiefs in 2023, becoming the first college athlete to do so. These experiences highlight her genuine love for sports beyond basketball.

Caitlin's humility and grounded nature are evident in her interactions with fans and the media. Despite her superstar status, she often downplays her achievements. At the Big Ten media day in October 2023, she remarked, "I think it's cool to see how excited people are. But at the same time, it takes you back like, I'm just a regular person. Like, I'm not that cool. I can just maybe score a basket or two." This modesty endears her to fans and serves as a reminder of her authentic character.

I apologize for the incomplete sentence in my previous response. Let's continue exploring Caitlin Clark's personal life and the individuals who have influenced her journey.

In December 2024, Caitlin Clark attended back-to-back Taylor Swift concerts at Lucas Oil Stadium in Indianapolis. She expressed her excitement on social media, sharing highlights from the event and mentioning how "fired up" she was to see Swift perform live. This experience not only showcased her love for music but also highlighted her ability to balance her professional commitments with personal enjoyment.

Clark's admiration for Swift extended beyond the concerts. She received a personal invitation from Swift to attend a Kansas City Chiefs game, further solidifying their budding friendship. Reflecting on this, Clark shared, "Taylor is obviously amazing, but I just think the coolest thing about her is her ability to bring people together and find joy in something."

Despite her rising fame, Clark remains deeply connected to her roots and values the relationships that have supported her journey. Her family's influence, her relationship with Connor McCaffery, and her diverse interests outside of basketball paint a picture of a well-rounded individual who cherishes the people and passions that enrich her life.

CHAPTER 5

THE ADVERSITIES THAT FUELED HER FIRE

Caitlin Clark's journey to basketball stardom has been marked by numerous challenges and obstacles that have tested her resilience and determination. From physical injuries to intense media scrutiny and on-court rivalries, Clark has faced each hurdle with unwavering resolve, turning adversities into fuel for her competitive fire.

Early Career Challenges

In her junior year at the University of Iowa, Clark encountered a significant setback. On November 18, 2022, during a closely contested game against Kansas State, she suffered an ankle injury with just 3.8 seconds remaining. Despite the injury, Clark had managed to contribute 27 points, 10 rebounds, and seven assists. Reflecting on this moment, she stated, "Injuries are part of the game. It's how you respond that defines you." Demonstrating her commitment, Clark returned to the court in the next game against Belmont on November 20, leading her team to victory with a remarkable 33-point performance. This episode highlighted her physical toughness and dedication to her team.

Navigating Professional Pressures

Transitioning to the WNBA, Clark's rookie season with the Indiana Fever in 2024 was fraught with challenges beyond the physical demands of the game. The heightened media attention and expectations placed immense pressure on her.

In an interview, she expressed, "The spotlight can be overwhelming, but I focus on my love for the game and my team's goals." This mindset allowed her to maintain focus amidst the external pressures.

On-Court Physicality and Rivalries

Clark's aggressive playing style often made her a target for physical play from opponents. In her first playoff appearance against the Connecticut Sun, she faced intense physical defense, including an incident where she sustained a black eye from DiJonai Carrington during Game 1. Despite the injury and the lack of a foul call, Clark continued to play, showcasing her toughness. She remarked, "Physical play is part of the game. You have to stand your ground and keep pushing forward." This resilience not only demonstrated her personal fortitude but also set a standard for her teammates.

Media Scrutiny and Controversies

Clark's prominence also subjected her to intense media scrutiny. In December 2024, after being named Time's Athlete of the Year, she addressed the perceived rivalry with fellow player Angel Reese. The media had amplified their on-court interactions, portraying a contentious relationship. Clark clarified, "The narrative about a rivalry is fabricated. Angel and I are competitors on the court, but there's mutual respect." By confronting these misconceptions directly, Clark aimed to shift the focus back to the sport and their respective achievements.

Addressing Racial Dynamics

Clark has also been candid about the racial dynamics within professional sports. In a December 2024 interview, she acknowledged her position, stating, "I want to say I've earned every single thing, but as a white person, there is privilege." This acknowledgment sparked both praise and criticism.

Some viewed her comments as a necessary recognition of systemic inequalities, while others perceived them as controversial. Clark responded to the backlash by emphasizing her intent to honor the contributions of Black athletes and to use her platform to advocate for equality. She stated, "It's about recognizing the realities of the world we live in and ensuring that those who came before me are acknowledged for their contributions." This perspective highlights her awareness of broader societal issues and her commitment to fostering inclusivity in sports.

Resilience Amidst Personal Attacks

Throughout her career, Clark has faced personal attacks and criticisms. During her rookie season, she was subjected to derogatory remarks from media personalities, including an incident where a commentator used a derogatory term to describe her on national television. Clark chose to rise above these insults, focusing on her performance and letting her achievements speak for themselves. She mentioned, "Criticism comes with the territory. I choose to focus on what I can control—my game and my growth." This approach underscores her mental toughness and ability to maintain composure under pressure.

Overcoming Team Dynamics and Performance Pressures

Adjusting to the professional league also required Clark to navigate team dynamics and performance expectations. The Indiana Fever, aiming to build a competitive team around her, made strategic roster changes, including signing veteran players to provide guidance and experience. Clark embraced these changes, stating, "Having seasoned players is invaluable. They bring experience and leadership that elevate the entire team." Balancing her role as a rising star with the integration of new teammates required adaptability and a team-first mentality.

Confronting Online Harassment

The digital age has brought about challenges of online harassment and abuse. Following playoff games, instances of racist and sexist comments directed at Clark and her teammates surfaced on social media platforms. The WNBA and fellow players condemned these actions, emphasizing the need for respect and inclusivity. Clark addressed the issue by focusing on unity and resilience, stating, "Hate has no place in our game. We stand together against all forms of discrimination." Her stance reinforced the importance of solidarity and maintaining focus amidst external negativity.

Learning from On-Court Mistakes

Clark's aggressive style of play, while a significant asset, also led to challenges such as turnovers and technical fouls. During her rookie season, she accumulated six technical fouls, bringing her close to a suspension. Reflecting on this, she acknowledged the need for emotional regulation, stating, "I think I could have done a better job keeping my emotions in check." This self-awareness and willingness to learn from mistakes highlight her commitment to personal growth and professionalism.

Balancing Personal Life and Professional Demands

Maintaining a balance between personal life and professional commitments posed another challenge for Clark. Despite her demanding schedule, she prioritized time with family and friends, often engaging in activities like golfing and attending concerts to unwind. She shared, "It's important to find time for yourself and your loved ones. It keeps you grounded."

CHAPTER 6

Net Worth & Endorsements – The Business of Being Caitlin Clark

Caitlin Clark's meteoric rise in the world of basketball has been accompanied by significant financial success, driven by her exceptional talent, marketability, and strategic partnerships. As of 2024, her estimated net worth is approximately $4 million, a testament to her achievements both on and off the court.

Earnings from the WNBA

In April 2024, Clark was selected as the first overall pick by the Indiana Fever in the WNBA Draft. Her four-year contract with the team is valued at $338,000, with annual salaries increasing each year. While this figure is substantial, it represents a fraction of her total earnings, highlighting the significant impact of her off-court ventures.

Endorsement Deals and Partnerships

Clark's marketability has attracted numerous high-profile endorsement deals, significantly contributing to her financial portfolio. In April 2024, she signed an eight-year contract with Nike valued at $28 million, marking one of the largest sponsorship deals for a women's basketball player. This agreement includes promotional appearances, product endorsements, and features in Nike's marketing campaigns.

Beyond Nike, Clark has secured partnerships with several other major brands:

- **Gatorade**: Clark has been featured in national commercials, and the company donated $22,000 to the Caitlin Clark Foundation in late 2023.

- **State Farm**: She became the first female athlete to be a spokesperson for State Farm, appearing in national television commercials.

- **Wilson Sporting Goods**: In May 2024, Clark signed a multiyear deal with Wilson, becoming the first athlete since Michael Jordan to release signature basketball collections with the company.

- **Panini America**: In March 2024, Clark signed a multiyear contract with the trading card company, becoming the first female athlete to have an exclusive partnership with Panini.

- **Gainbridge**: She signed a multiyear sponsorship with the Indianapolis-based financial platform, joining Billie Jean King and Annika Sörenstam as brand ambassadors.

These partnerships not only provide substantial financial compensation but also enhance Clark's visibility and influence across various industries.

Philanthropy and Community Engagement

Despite her burgeoning wealth, Clark remains committed to giving back to her community. In March 2022, she partnered with the Coralville Community Food Pantry in Coralville,

Iowa, for a month-long donation drive and meet-and-greet event called "Team Up Against Hunger." The initiative raised over $23,000 for the food pantry in its first year. A year later, Clark and the pantry teamed up again, raising over $75,000 in thirty days. As of 2024, Clark has helped raise over $100,000 for the Coralville Community Food Pantry.

In October 2023, Clark established the Caitlin Clark Foundation, a nonprofit organization dedicated to uplifting and improving the lives of youth and their communities through education, nutrition, and sport. Beneficiaries of the foundation include The Boys and Girls Clubs of Central Iowa and the Coralville Community Food Pantry. Many of Clark's sponsorship and endorsement deals include pledges of support or monetary donations to the foundation. For instance, as part of her multiyear deal with Gatorade, the company donated $22,000 to the Caitlin Clark Foundation in late 2023.

In January 2025, on her 23rd birthday, the Caitlin Clark Foundation partnered with Scholastic and their national literacy program, United States of Readers, to donate 22,000 books to under-resourced elementary and middle schools in both Iowa and Indiana.

Financial Management and Future Prospects

Clark's financial success is a result of strategic planning and prudent management. Her substantial endorsement deals have provided a steady income stream, allowing her to invest in various ventures and philanthropic efforts. By aligning herself with reputable brands and causes, Clark has not only enhanced her financial standing but also solidified her position as a role model and influencer.

Looking ahead, Clark's financial trajectory appears promising. Her continued success in the WNBA, coupled with her expanding portfolio of endorsement deals and philanthropic initiatives, positions her for sustained financial growth. As she continues to leverage her platform and influence, Clark is poised to make a lasting impact both within and beyond the realm of sports.

CHAPTER 7

HOW SHE CHANGED THE GAME FOREVER

Caitlin Clark's journey through the world of basketball has not only been one of unparalleled achievement but also one of profound influence. Through her incredible skills on the court, her leadership, and the way she carries herself off the court, Clark has changed the landscape of women's basketball forever. From her record-breaking college career at Iowa to her rise as a professional player in the WNBA, she has become a symbol of inspiration, resilience, and change for both athletes and fans worldwide.

Her impact stretches beyond statistics, and her legacy is not solely defined by the titles, records, and trophies she has accumulated. It's about how she has fundamentally altered the game of basketball, especially for women. When you look at Caitlin Clark, what stands out is how her skills, particularly her shooting range and playmaking ability, have redefined what is possible for a female player. Widely regarded as one of the greatest women's college basketball players of all time, Caitlin has pushed the boundaries of what is considered a "good shot." Her ability to shoot from deep beyond the three-point line has changed the dimensionality of the game, with some even comparing her impact to that of NBA star Stephen Curry. Just as Curry transformed how men's basketball is played with his long-range shooting, Caitlin Clark has done the same for women's basketball, forcing teams to adjust their strategies and creating an entirely new dynamic for the game.

What makes Caitlin's influence even more profound is the attention she's brought to women's basketball. Through her stellar performances, she has sparked what has been coined the "Caitlin Clark Effect." It's not just about the increased viewership and the packed arenas at Iowa; it's about how she has brought a mainstream audience to a sport that once struggled for recognition. In her senior season, the women's basketball program at Iowa sold out every game, generating a record $3.26 million in ticket sales. Caitlin didn't just fill the stands at her home games; she brought in millions of viewers on TV. The national championship game in 2024, which Caitlin played in, broke viewership records, drawing 18.9 million viewers. It was the most-watched basketball game at any level since 2019, even surpassing the men's NCAA final in viewership.

Her influence didn't stop with the college game. As Caitlin entered the WNBA, she continued to drive record-breaking attendance and viewership. In her first season with the Indiana Fever, she helped set the franchise's single-season attendance record and made history with the highest attendance in a WNBA game. The Fever's regular season finale saw 20,711 fans in the stands—an attendance record for the league. Caitlin's star power and influence are undeniable, and they've made waves across the sports world. But her effect doesn't stop at just numbers. It's about how she has opened doors for future generations of women's basketball players, showing them that it is possible to dream bigger, to be bold, and to achieve greatness on a scale once thought impossible for female athletes.

Caitlin's success has also sparked important conversations about race and gender in sports. As her popularity soared, some members of her fan base, particularly those who were new to the sport, engaged in harmful behaviors, including racist, sexist, and homophobic harassment of fellow players. This abuse was most apparent in the wake of Caitlin's rookie season with the Fever, where opposing teams not only committed hard fouls on her but also downplayed her achievements. The media scrutiny that Caitlin faced as a woman in a male-dominated sport was harsh, and it was compounded by the targeted hate she received online. But Caitlin's response to this adversity spoke volumes about her character. She denounced the abuse, making it clear that those who engaged in such behavior were not true fans of the game. She called them trolls and stood firm in her belief that the spotlight should be on the game and the players, not on divisive rhetoric.

Her stance on the matter helped bring much-needed attention to the way women athletes are treated, especially in the media. Caitlin refused to be silenced by the negativity and instead continued to play the game with the same fire and determination that made her a star in the first place. She refused to let the hatred of a few dictate her journey, and instead, she used it as fuel to keep pushing forward, both on and off the court. Her courage in the face of adversity only solidified her legacy as a trailblazer and a true role model for young athletes everywhere.

But Caitlin's influence extends beyond the basketball court and into the larger world of sports culture. Her success has had a ripple effect on how women's basketball is perceived. She has shown the world that women athletes are not just capable of playing at the highest level—they are capable of dominating the sport. She's challenged long-standing stereotypes about women's athleticism and rewritten the narrative about what women in sports can achieve. For Caitlin, it has always been about proving that female athletes deserve the same respect, the same recognition, and the same opportunities as their male counterparts. She's paved the way for future female athletes to dream bigger, to go further, and to reach the heights that were once reserved for men.

Off the court, Caitlin has used her platform to advocate for gender equality in sports. She has spoken out about the disparities between women's and men's sports, including the unequal pay, media coverage, and overall treatment of female athletes. Caitlin has emphasized that the work isn't done yet—that there's still a long way to go before women's sports receive the attention and respect they deserve. But she remains hopeful, knowing that the next generation of female athletes will be able to build on the foundation that she and others have laid. She's not just changing the game for herself; she's doing it for every girl who picks up a basketball and dreams of greatness.

Her legacy is also felt through the impact she's had on the players she's inspired. For many young girls, Caitlin Clark represents the epitome of hard work, passion, and perseverance. Her story is a testament to what can be achieved when you commit to your dreams and give everything you have. She has become a beacon of hope for young athletes, showing them that with the right mindset, anything is possible. Caitlin has often expressed how much she loves seeing young girls look up to her and how proud she is to be a role model. She's conscious of the responsibility that comes with her platform and uses it to motivate the next generation to reach higher and go further.

Caitlin's influence on the game is undeniable, but so is her impact on her community. She has consistently given back, using her platform to raise awareness for various charitable causes. Her work with organizations like the Boys & Girls Clubs of Central Iowa and the Coralville Community Food Pantry shows her deep commitment to giving back and making a difference. Caitlin has always been clear about her values, and it's no surprise that her legacy extends beyond the court. Her influence is felt not just by basketball fans but by the countless individuals she's helped through her philanthropic efforts.

As Caitlin continues her career, her impact only grows. She remains dedicated to using her platform to bring about change, advocating for women's sports, encouraging young athletes, and giving back to the communities that supported her from the start. Her story is one of perseverance, determination, and passion. She has redefined what it means to be a woman in sports, leaving a legacy that will inspire generations to come.

Caitlin's legacy is secure, but her journey is far from over. The world of women's basketball is forever changed by her talent, her leadership, and her unwavering belief in herself and the game. As she continues to play, to inspire, and to break barriers, Caitlin Clark's influence will only grow, shaping the future of sports for years to come.

AUTHOR'S PERSPECTIVE

WHY CAITLIN CLARK'S STORY MATTERS

Writing a biography is not something I thought I would ever do, let alone write about someone I admire so much. But Caitlin Clark's story deserves to be told. It deserves to be remembered. I have followed her journey for years, from her first days on the court at Iowa to her rise as one of the most electrifying players in women's basketball. As a fan, it's impossible not to be captivated by her resilience, her undeniable talent, and the way she has completely changed the game. This biography isn't authorized, and it's not a story told by someone close to Caitlin herself, but as someone who's watched her career with awe and admiration, I felt compelled to share why her story matters.

It's not just about basketball. It's about breaking barriers, defying expectations, and showing the world what women in sports can truly achieve. Caitlin Clark has done something rare in the world of sports: she has turned her passion into something that transcends the court. Watching her play isn't just about seeing a player score points; it's about witnessing someone push the boundaries of what's possible and challenge the status quo of women's sports. Caitlin isn't just a player; she's a symbol, a beacon of hope for young athletes everywhere, showing them that the road to greatness is theirs to carve, no matter how hard the journey may be.

I've watched her rise from a young, ambitious athlete to a superstar in college basketball, and now, as she continues to shine in the WNBA, her impact grows every day. She isn't just breaking records—she's reshaping the game. Caitlin has proven that women's basketball isn't just a side note in the world of sports; it's powerful, it's thrilling, and it can captivate an audience in ways never seen before. Every game she plays feels like a new chapter in the evolution of the sport. I remember watching her in the national championship game, where millions of eyes were on her, and for the first time, women's basketball felt like it was on the same level as men's basketball. That's the Caitlin Clark effect. That's the difference she's making, and it's something I will never forget.

But why write this biography? Why dedicate so much time to a story that isn't mine to tell? For me, it's because Caitlin's journey is about more than just basketball—it's about what it means to push through doubt, to face adversity head-on, and to do so with grace, determination, and authenticity. I wanted to capture that. I wanted others to understand what makes Caitlin Clark so special, not just as an athlete but as a person. Her ability to rise above criticism, the strength she shows in the face of adversity, and the way she handles the spotlight with humility are qualities we should all strive for. She has faced so many challenges in her career, from injury to intense media scrutiny, and through it all, she has come out stronger, more determined, and more focused on the game she loves. Her resilience is a lesson in itself.

In telling Caitlin's story, I also wanted to remind readers that this biography is not an authorized one. It's not written with direct input from Caitlin or her inner circle. Instead, it's written from the perspective of a fan, someone who has watched her and admired her from afar. I've never had the privilege of speaking with Caitlin directly, but that doesn't diminish the respect I have for her. This biography is a reflection of how she's inspired me, how she's influenced the sports world, and how she's touched the lives of so many others who watch her play. I wanted to share the story of Caitlin Clark from a place of admiration, with the hope that others can feel the same sense of awe I do every time I watch her play.

Caitlin's story matters because it isn't just hers—it belongs to every young girl who dreams of playing sports, to every athlete who's been told they're not good enough, and to every person who has been knocked down but refuses to stay down. Caitlin has shown us all what it means to fight for what you want and to do so unapologetically. She hasn't just overcome obstacles; she's used them to fuel her fire. Every setback, every piece of criticism, every hard fall has only made her stronger and more determined to succeed. That's the kind of story worth telling. That's why Caitlin Clark's story matters.

One of the things that's most inspiring about Caitlin is the way she handles the weight of being a role model. It's something that can't be easy, especially at such a young age. But Caitlin doesn't shy away from the responsibility. She understands the power her platform has, and she uses it to advocate for women in sports, for equality, and for the next generation of athletes. When she's asked about her influence, she never talks about herself as a star. Instead, she talks about the game and how important it is for women to have the same opportunities as men. She's not just playing for herself; she's playing for every woman who has been overlooked or underestimated. She is aware of the responsibility she carries, and she carries it with grace and humility.

In interviews, Caitlin has expressed her desire to inspire young athletes, saying, "I just want to show girls that they can do anything they want. It's all about believing in yourself and not letting anyone tell you that you can't achieve something." That belief in herself is what sets her apart. She's made history, broken records, and transformed the game of basketball, but more than that, she's given countless young girls the courage to believe in their dreams. She's shown them that they are capable of achieving greatness, no matter the obstacles they might face.

Her impact is also felt through the countless young athletes who now look up to her. Caitlin has become a beacon of hope for so many girls who want to play sports, who want to be seen and heard, and who want to have the same opportunities as boys. Her presence in the WNBA has helped increase the visibility of women's basketball, and as she continues to break barriers, she opens the door for more women to step into the spotlight. But Caitlin's influence goes beyond basketball. She has inspired a generation of young women to push for equality in all aspects of life, whether it's in sports, business, or any other field.

One of the most touching moments of Caitlin's career came when she was asked about her relationship with her family and how they had supported her. She shared that her parents, Brent and Anne, were always there for her, from driving her to practices when she was a little girl to supporting her every step of the way in her career. Caitlin's relationship with her family is one of the cornerstones of her success. They've been her biggest supporters, and in turn, she's used her platform to lift them up. Caitlin's spouse, Connor McCaffery, has also been an important part of her journey. Their relationship has been a source of strength for Caitlin, and she often speaks about how much he has helped her maintain balance in her life. "Having someone who understands the pressure of being a student-athlete has been invaluable," Caitlin has said about Connor. Their partnership is a reminder that no one achieves greatness alone, and the people who love and support you are just as important as the work you put in yourself.

As you read Caitlin's story, I hope you see the same things I do. I hope you see a young woman who has never let anything stop her from reaching her goals. I hope you see someone who has taken the challenges of her career and turned them into opportunities for growth. Most of all, I hope you see someone who is more than just a basketball player. She's a trailblazer, an advocate, and a role model for everyone who dares to dream big. Caitlin Clark's story is a testament to the power of perseverance, belief in oneself, and the importance of lifting others up along the way. She is living proof that with hard work and determination, anything is possible.

In the end, Caitlin's legacy will not only be defined by the records she's broken or the accolades she's earned but by the lives she's touched and the barriers she's shattered. She will always be remembered as a player who changed the game, but more importantly, she'll be remembered as someone who inspired a generation to reach for the stars and believe in their own potential.

As I reflect on her journey, I'm reminded of her own words: "If you want something, you have to go get it. No one's going to hand it to you." That's the spirit that defines Caitlin Clark, and it's a message we should all carry with us.

Made in the USA
Monee, IL
16 May 2025